INSOMNIAC'S LULLABY

INSOMNIAC'S LULLABY

SARAH
LINDSAY

To Michael
from Sarah Lindsay
with thanks for the reading
1/11/98

1989

Unicorn Press, Inc.   Greensboro, N.C.

Also by Sarah Lindsay:
Bodies of Water   (Unicorn Press, 1986)

Prints by Jane Blocker

Poems that were published in *The Annunciation,*
Blue Pitcher, The Greensboro Review, International Poetry Review
and *Omega News* are reprinted with permission.

Library of Congress Cataloguing-in-Publication Data:

Lindsay, Sarah, 1958-
    Insomniac's Lullaby.

    I. Title.
PS3562.I51192I57   1989   811'.54   89-4870
ISBN 0-87775-221-4

Unicorn Press, Inc.
P.O. Box 3307
Greensboro, N.C. 27402

TABLE OF CONTENTS

THE STABILITY OF MOVING OBJECTS

The stability of moving objects has become my study,
as in How long will this furry infant leaf,
nipped by the wiper blade, ride on my windshield?
Let the car's acceleration be x, let my destination be y,
let the sudden car turned in my path be d---
(my right arm gate-swings across the empty seat
as if born to a mother). How far will my purse tumble?
At what speed around this corner will the brownbag lunch
subside from its tentative upright?
                    Adept at solutions, I may in time proceed
to the calculus of infinite variables—the arc of an attention span,
how far a body can bend, how its juices settle,
how far two people are flung if they suddenly stop.
The ice scraper slides to a halt on the dash.
By the front steps a white kitten preps the next experiment,
paw hook, lunge. It has a thumb-size beetle at bay,
now flipped, watched narrowly, cuffed and evaded.
How stable is a beetle on its back.

THE GIRL IN THE WAITING ROOM

I won't think about the needle
spraying rotten-banana juice
and zinging hot wires from my gums through my eyes.
They'll buy me a milkshake after.
And I'll ask for the teeth in a little snap-plastic box
again, it holds nickels not quarters and snaps
open and shut, the teeth rattle like toys.
I like things little, that fit in one hand,
pick the smallest doll, the smallest dragon teacup,
the babiest clay dogs, tiny notebooks.
I want if the house burns down to be able to carry out
everything that matters in a grocery sack.
The teeth that came out themselves were hollow chips,
looked like they couldn't chew, but that last molar
he wrenched out—crack—
that one left a hole. It had three roots,
three long roots. For a tooth.
It's in my jewelry box. I'll keep them all
one way or another.
My hands are sweaty.

ANTENNA SOUND

The caller, whose third ring I have interrupted to say hello,
says nothing. Not even a foolish obscenity. Not even breathing.
A fizz on the line, like the air in the next room but one,
means connection yet. At 7 : 30 a.m.,
clearly someone is trying to steal my soul, like a white man photographer
who catches them in a box. I feel it despite me
begin to creep out in threads over the wire.

And I'd sent down the shower drain in a clockwise spiral
all I can spare today. Later the radio
turns sly; the jockey's voice pauses expectantly
and doesn't glide on, but no music plays,
no advertisement rattles its bars. Antenna sound
sucks the inside of my ears.
Better to hear the traffic, better to mutter disgust
at the sleek car that speeds past mine
than to think of space, without air to bear the sun.
If you go out unsuitably clothed it pulls out your lungs,
because they wanted to breathe so badly they were empty.

(Dining with her unsuspecting parents she orders clams)

At this lovely restaurant with Mother, with Dad,
with not you, I meant to drown
my expensive sorrows in a dish of clams: fried
clams that come in a silver bowl lined with lettuce,
lined with very dew—air-conditioned—
but you're so like clams à la carte.
There is a silver cup in the silver bowl
like you-within-you, engaging as Russian dolls
and scary—will the next one be empty?—the cup
richly filled with red sauce, whose horseradish
catches the back of my throat like your voice
fiercely whispering in the front seat, dim
between the street lights. Whose ketchup tang
is your impossible hair, also called red, which also
catches the back of my throat. I think I want
to eat it. So bright. Then we have the lemon
wedge, like a halfhearted moon. Some moons
turn us into shadows, some only hang
drearily over the empty street while l drive home,
racing the sun-clearing-its-throat to the bed
I haven't been to yet. I squeeze the lemon
gently, let one drop fall at a time glistening
on a chosen clam. These are your tears,
pale colorless yellow with a bite, oh nothing
tastes quite like irony foreseen but unavoidable.
That's how your tears were. The puckered wedge
is your last weak smile, which I took whole—gently—
in my mouth, which is why I pucker now,
it may be permanent. Notice the elegant
pale pink plastic sword thrust neatly
through the heart of the heartless lemon. A halved seed
drops silent as a jewel into the cupped hands
of the praying lettuce, which still offers me
a handful of curled cuddled fried fattening
succulent unchewable swallowmewhole golden brown plump—
I accept with dubious appetite. Tomorrow we meet
again, in secret, again, again.

RUMINATION

Your red leaf pressed
in my thickest book of stories
holds it shut. I suspect
the leaf died brown
and all the words run red
but I won't look.
Suppose I broke the paper spine,
found whole pages falling dry
for wind to scuttle away,
and one serrated oval
waiting perfectly, sharpened.

Still, one must mark the important places, that's what
scars are for I always say.
Only we should have been safely labeled then—
CAUTION
HARMFUL IF SWALLOWED
KEEP OUT OF REACH OF CHILDREN
Instead with a year's spring fever
we nipped at our own hands bound out of reach
and discovered a taste for each other.

Monday I want to apologize,
Tuesday to rock you to sleep,
Wednesday I try eating chocolate
but my tastes have grown too refined;
I want a mouthful of glass,
pure slick to my tongue as diamond,
crystal clean prisms
and blades to bite down on —
nothing else delivers
that crunch between the teeth,
those bright slivers.

TERMS

Haunted is hunted with mouth open wide.
Night is nigh with a tap on the wall.
Ghost is guest and host, takes your room
and makes you stay till he goes.
Moon is the small sound from you
that fails to lighten silence.
Wait is when your legs are too heavy to move,
stare is the air hissing between your faces,
hiss is kiss with the touch stripped away.
Sigh: sight unfocused.
Depart means
he is reburied, deep in your chest.

Figure one: the X babies
one and a half months old.
Two heads, two arms, three legs,
a tangle of ribs and belly.
Their eyes tight shut, they are either
crying or yawning, fisting their little
ten fingers and fifteen toes.

Figure two: line drawing,
free of shadows, squirms,
wrinkles, mouths. A dotted line
mapped on their middle
winds like a river,
worming out the normal lives
the doctor wants them to lead.

Figure three: a chart in tiny type
with baby asterisks. Permanent scorecard:
who got what. Brothers and sisters share.

"*A* showed more assertiveness,
we found, than *B*. We gave him the scrotum
and two legs. Later
we can make her a false vagina."

Figure four: the X babies
stitched in two healing pieces,
eyes wide open,
staring at each other.

INSOMNIAC'S LULLABY

Lie down and worry.
Close eyes and stare.
Someone must count all the ways to take care.

Beware the sleep of the stove's blue eye
Or the wink of a spark on a cord.
Too much heat could be fire, disguised
As the line of light under the door.
If the line's gone dark, do you hear the step
Of someone who thinks you're asleep?
It could be a thief, or your neighbor still up.
It could be your neighbor's a thief.

You shouldn't have said what you said to him but
You should have said something to her.
You meant to buy something but not what you bought
And you put it down somewhere, but where?
The plumbing still leaks—hear a drop hear a drop—
You may not have emptied the bowl.
A siren is yelling now close now it stops
But was it an ambulance, fire, or the cops,
And was it on time?
                    What's the time?
Are you getting old?

It's quiet. Too quiet. Too noisy before.
You can hear the sick sound in the hall
Of nobody coming to knock on your door,
Of something not happening, midnight or morning,
Nothing here happening at all.

Lie down and worry.
Close eyes and stare.
Someone must count all the reasons to fear.

EYES

Sullen potatoes in the drawer inch out white feelers,
onions nested in plastic thrust white-green tusks from their middles.
Cuttings have filled their wet cups on the sill with white tangle
and under their heart-shaped leaves stretch out curved, brown scaly
fingers, one tip to the pane, one pointing gradually down.
A cobweb hangs from the ceiling by one end.
On the bed a sheet covers her starfish arms and legs, her splayed hands.
Not water, not air. All I know is I can't reach it.

TREMOR

Pick up this house and shake it.
First out is the old lady, the holes in her chest
almost burned through, her mouth full of cigarettes.
She has packed all her gardens in trunks, she has written her memoirs.
She was expecting you.
Next out the man with an armful of books,
waving the one with his thumb in, wait till I finish.
Then the two daughters caught changing their clothes,
limply holding the first pan or umbrella they saw,
each crying the same boy's name before hearing the other.
The cat steps to the window,
licks its fur down to a new color
and goes back in
where the third girl is pacing from room to room barefoot,
shaking her hands like maracas,
singing out like the toppled piano
the lump that's been looming up from her chest to her throat
for days. Is it an egg or a bubble?
Pick up this house and shake it, she hisses,
crouched ready to dance on the walls.

ELLIPSES

It's closer to the earth tonight,
That bunged-up prehistoric satellite,
Tugging cold water blankets close
Over the shoulders of the shores,
Tickling those disposed to be mad
As hairs rise singly slightly from their heads

Its gravity is levity down here,
Its luminance makes objects disappear,
And someone on an aimless walk
Feels her skull pull straight its mooring neck,
Remembers as her wrists rise from her sides
Whatever orbits, flies

MOONS OF JUPITER

On the waste of my own table
past my elbow and wet rings,
two crumbs.
One is white,
one is almost yellow.
From lunch? last night? how long
have they been orbiting,
seed pearls barely round enough
for shadows? Two points
of infinite angles,
transients apparently still.

Come see the moons of Jupiter,
Daddy said.
We strolled out for the show
to the long Antarctic ice cream telescope
gleaming night white in the yard
as he deftly fed it bright numbers,
netting scoops of sky.
My turn was slip up a soundless chute
into weightless blue
(not lighter than air, as light)
where noble Jupiter
whirled a silver bola by his head.
The shining disc stood from the night
while little sparks as echoes of his edge
turned on magnetic strings.
(Close up in Daddy's magazine
they looked like baked potatoes,
inset in a portrait of the king.)
Neat, Dad, each daughter said,
and till our planet shouldered them from view
we watched the moons of Jupiter swing
as if he might let them go.

TWINS

I stand on my head on your head.
No one applauds.
Sometimes I pretend
I can comb my hair
and you are not what parts it,
but only my ponytail.
Sometimes you wag me.
All day you are the one right-side up.
At night I make you dream
you walk on the sky.
I am the only girl you can't have.
Yours are the only eyes I'll never meet.

GRAPEFRUIT LOVE

Sometimes between the first pucker and last grimace
you are sweet to me, grapefruit love, my little menace.
With each morning's opening acid wince,
our mutual sharp ministrations begin in suspense—
will you pinch my eye, or blind it, spoil my food for me,
or give your all in a flurry of being good for me?
be stickily dry, or generous in torrents?
More elusive than lemonade's, more dearly bought than orange's
the sweetness I dig for again and again, my sweet,
to be late for work always, and wishing I'd brushed my teeth.

DECOMPRESSION

The destined, magnified couple trip lightly over obstacles of plot
                                        and propriety,
reminiscing, kissing, undressing,
and their movie throws a simple, dignified bedsheet over their lack
                                        of restraint,
accordion-pleats and serenades the long sweaty enjambment
into twenty seconds of R-rated sublimity above her clavicle and his ribs.

Those of us fed on montage, pruned scenes in pruned stories,
where music swells over mere sounds of voices and traffic
and camera-clean cuts tuck flab,
enter the parking lot springily
but falter a little over painted lines and stamped circles of gum,
still nursing the sense of frame center, but profile or full face?
                                        Now, or now?
And the looming nine-tenths of viciously ordinary iceberg
                                        approaches our boats.

HEART SPINNING

fat wedge on its tip
with a gyroscope hum,
on a blue and red stick
my heart spun

doing its job
like a second-hand's tick,
a solid-blur top

one finger
snapped the spell—
I won't say it fell

but at your touch
the spin went wide,
drew drunken circles
side to side

an hourglass twist
bobbed in my chest

look what you've done—
a waver wobble
in the hum

and a skip
on the tip

SESTINA THAT CHEWS ON ITSELF

A poem
boxed in a game,
a checkerboard
run through a sieve,
a deck of cards
with its tail in its mouth—

Tail in its mouth,
the poem
ticks like shuffled cards,
like hourglass sand, a game
of chess on a sieve's
checkerboard

of invisible sucking squares. Bored?
On the tip of my tongue, this tail in my mouth,
to say so, but that indecisive
organ waits as the poem
still boxes gamely
with its deck of words.

After all, I dealt the cards,
wound up the checkerboard.
To stop this music-box game
halfway between its tail and its mouth
would hang it in mid-air, mid-page, a choked poem,
a one-hole sieve.

Sponge cells, run through a sieve,
reassemble their self-same hand of cards,
their favorite one-word poem,
the only square they know on the checkerboard.
The sponge's tail is its mouth.
Blob of self, an unopened, unlost game.

Once opened, the box is too small for the game.
Disarranged, the parts swell, turn elusive,
their tails no longer fit in their mouths.
Refitting the dice, the tokens, fake money, bright houses, chance cards
is like refolding a road map, not a Monopoly board;
the rules turn into a poem

And the poem says, Try to pass Go on a checkerboard,
hold good luck in a deck of cards, or a sieve.
Try saying ''It's only a game'' with your heart in your mouth.

MARRIAGE OPTICS

When you look at me,
two of me just this high flip upside down
and float one in each eye (warm blue inside too),
it's like flying above cloud-fur cover with the sun before Christmas,
watched by the double round rainbow beyond the plane's wing,
and it's what I've always wanted, to swim in a sea
that tastes like water, like air,
like something besides my own spit.

When the little two of me fly through your head
and in unison turn right-side up
to be nuzzled by welcoming synapses,
it's like circling over O'Hare tonight after Christmas,
over its silver and firepink diamonds
in the lighted dark, all full of intention,
and it's what I've wanted, to gloat over all of them,
love them all luminous since one will be you when I land

and twos of us fall in each other as fast as we can

SATURDAY FAIRY TALE

Early morning curtain-filtered magnifies
perfectly
the first thing I see
if I wake before I must
but will not tell me what
is it
your nostril fringed with intimate eyelash hairs
the folded flesh fingerprint of your ear
    with its flush of private sunrise
your eyelid lightly creased, hiding indigo

Sleep beast has released me
only to bring it the first thing I see
Its horse now bears me back
down whatever tunnel my open eye fell in

Later the quick animal crossing my path
is your iris, testing me
for something recognizable
Leading me from the thicket of your beard

Impale me on each hair and finger of you
till from a great distance I find at last your face

The property of density

is the property of space:
Between any two points is a point.
This is the rule
of lines between lines on a ruler,
half, quarter, eighth, sixteenth,
thirty-second, sixty-fourth.
In an atom of air
there is room—not room for air,
but for a point.
And a point beside it.
And a point between.
And a point between that point
and each of the first two.
It's diving into a rabbit's hole
and when the sides scrape your skin
there's room for a point between.
It's playing the violin
with a note between any two fingers,
a note on either side.
"Subtlety knows no limit,"
Yehudi says, doing knee bends,
finger flexes, eating a pear,
recalling Dorati's mother, interned,
who played Beethoven quartets in her head
and stayed sane. Between his chin
and the chinrest, infinite points,
between his hand and the string.
For the moment none of us hear them.

PRAYER POSITION

It's too much to ask that you should speak
to me—
You, the intricate space between two blue porcelain horses,
the light past the leg of a dead cricket left on the rug,
the air on a chair standing gray in an almost black room,
the place I rise toward at night
       where two walls fit ceiling.
My ears unfurl from my head a little, sometimes.
Hear the creak in their circulation,
the hum around windows.
I mumble I'm listening, I'm listening,
and tell myself hush.

＊

Sarah Lindsay designed *Insomniac's Lullaby*, hand-set it
in 12 pt Perpetua type, printed it (with David Nikias)
on acid-free 70 # Mohawk Vellum
with a Vandercook SP15 hand press, and sewed
and bound it by hand. She wishes
to thank Jane Blocker, David Nikias,
and the Blue Pitcher poetry group, and to dedicate
this book to Teo Savory and Alan Brilliant.

)